MW01152365

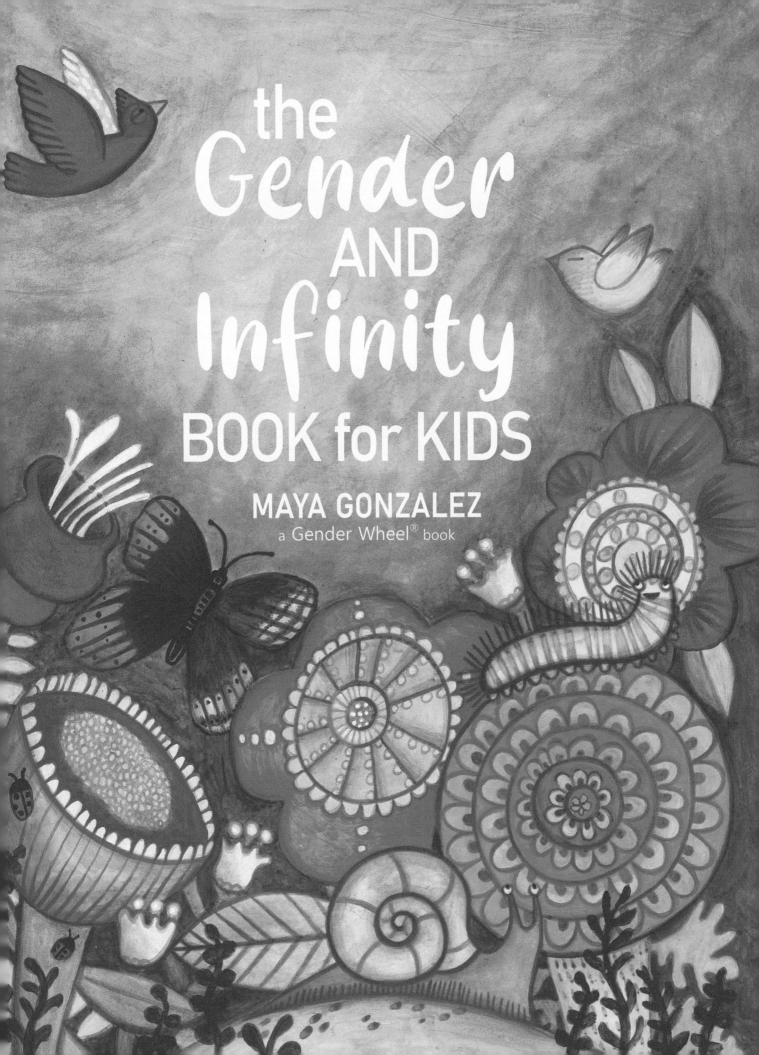

the Gender AND Infinity BOOK for KIDS

MAYA GONZALEZ

a Gender Wheel® book

Everything

Flowing,

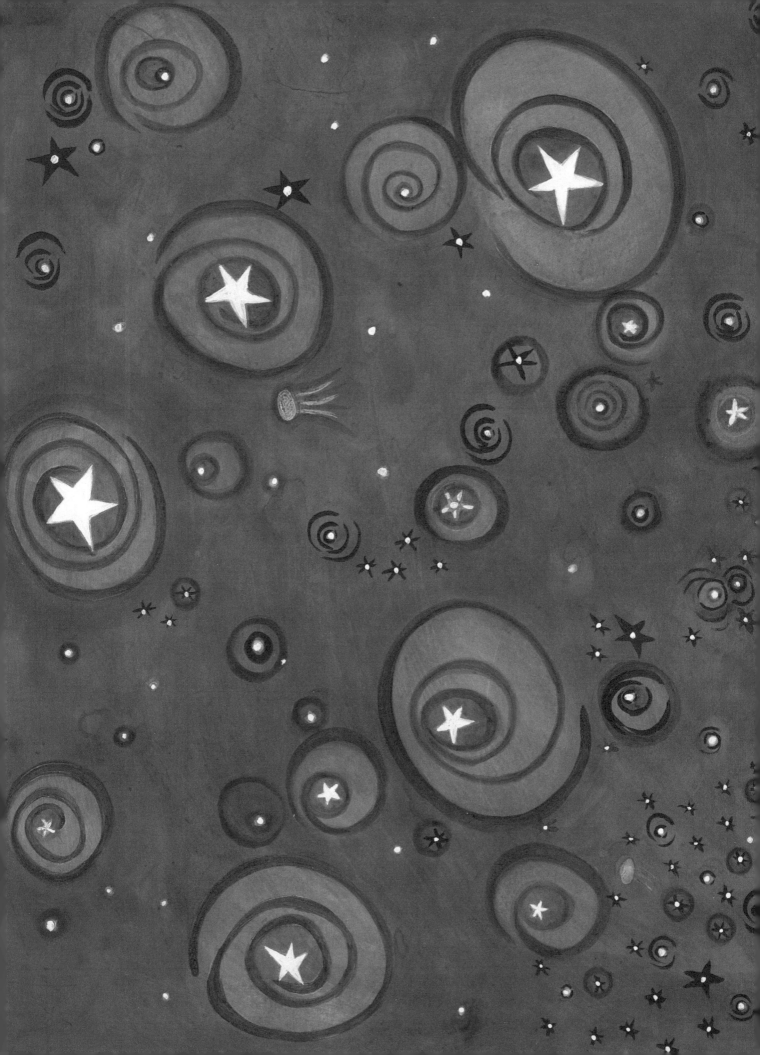

Everything Glowing.

and **Showing,**

and **Knowing.**

Everyone everywhere, inside and outside, is a part of infinity ...Going.

Then there are
THE BOXES.

People have been taught there are
TWO BOXES
**and everyone and everything must fit
into one or the other.**

It begins even before a person is born.

People ask,

"ARE YOU HAVING A BOY OR A GIRL?"

Why do they want to know?

They want to know because
THE BOX isn't just about the body
a person is born with.

It is also about how that body is expected
to look, act and feel inside,
even how that person is treated.

THE BOXES are based on old, small ideas and not on Nature's *infinity*.

Because of these ideas
people teach kids to fit into
one of **THE BOXES**
as they grow up.

People do this in
a million, little ways:

how they dress kids,
what toys they give them,
how people talk to kids
even how they play with them.

When kids are taught
to fit into **ONE BOX,**
it can be difficult to
see infinity.
THE BOXES
become everything.

And everything,
including our self
can get very, very
small and tight
to fit inside
THE BOX.

But even when **infinity** has been pushed inside THE BOX, **girl**

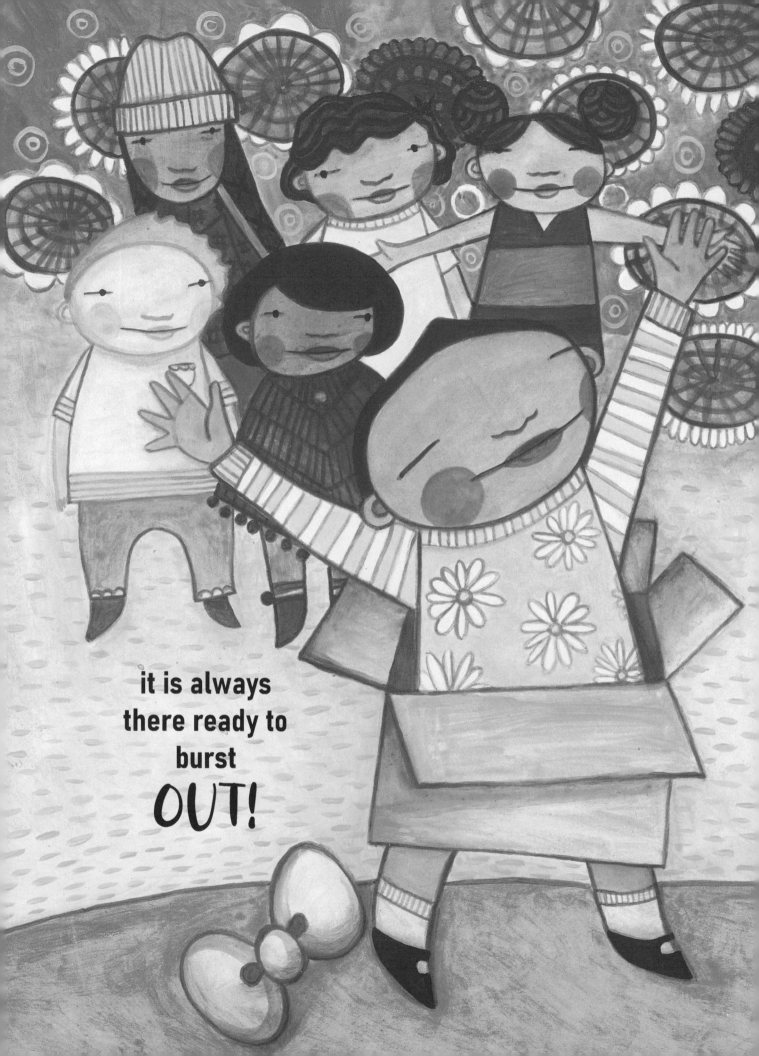

it is always
there ready to
burst
OUT!

Learning to
see Nature's
infinity
frees us from
the boxes.

Then everyone and everything can *flow* and **grow** in their own best way.

This is
who we are.
This is who we will
always BE.
Infinity.

Learning to See Nature's Infinity

Similar Patterns of Body, Gender, and Relationship Diversity exist across all realms of Nature

MEET THE KIDS! They are an important part of infinity. The kids are shown with their assignments to help us see that there are lots of different ways to be on the outside and feel on the inside beyond the boxes.

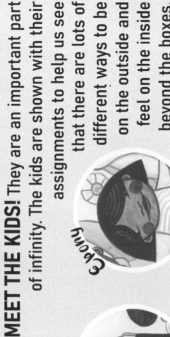

Ebony
THEY
assigned boy box

Diego
THEY
assigned boy box

Yoli
THEY
assigned boy box

Nikita
THEY
assigned girl box

Nathan
HE
assigned boy box

Asu
HE
assigned boy box

Ernesto
HE
assigned girl box

Maria
HE and SHE
assigned boy box

Gia
SHE
intersex/assigned boy box

Can you figure out the secret message using the first letter of each kid's name?

PLANTS like trees, flowers, fruits, herbs, nuts and more have a wide range of bodies and ways to reproduce using pollination with seeds and pollen, or spores.

Fruit
intersex: a body that is beyond male or female categories but still are assigned to one box

Flower
THEY
assigned boy box

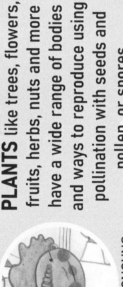

Tree
TREE
intersex/assigned girl box

Sky
HE
assigned girl box

River
SHE
intersex/assigned boy box

Coral
ALL PRONOUNS
assigned girl box

some plant bodies are both male and female and self-pollinate like roses, lilies, watermelon and mangos, and some trees change how they pollinate over time

AQUATIC LIFE has abundant and fluid diversity that includes natural body changes and ways to reproduce and care for young and even variations in behavior.

California sheepshead Wrasse

all begin as female, with one they all become male

Clownfish

if the female parent dies, the male parent changes to female

Coral

some of the longest living animals on earth self-fertilize

©2023 Maya Gonzalez | *The Gender and Infinity Book for Kids* | WWW.GENDERWHEEL.COM

BIRDS of all kinds have diverse body types, behaviors, and relationships.
Some have a portion of the body that is female and another portion that is male. Sometimes this is visible on the outside and sometimes it is not.

ANIMALS like reptiles, amphibians, and mammals are incredibly different, but they all have diversity in common. From lizards to lions there is no one way to behave "male" or "female." And many animals adapt and change in order to thrive.

Beluga — some have a body that is both male and female

Seahorse — males carry developing offspring and give birth

Bottlenose Dolphin — males form lifelong bonds with other males

Bigeye Houndshark — some females externally appear male

Bell Bird — many females have male features and behaviors

Cardinal — a few are visibly half male (red) and half female (white)

Penguin — some females partner with each other to raise young, as do males

Chicken — many females look like males

Hummingbird

Frog — have adaptive bodies that can change from male to female when necessary

Whiptail Lizard — all are female and reproduce by parthenogenesis, similar to self-fertilization

Giraffe

Boa — some have a body with a mosaic of male and female features

Cat

Monkey — many kinds form strong male/male bonds and female/female bonds

Lion — a group of females look and behave exactly like males

Black Maned Lion

Bear — some Grizzly, Black and Polar bears have a body that is both male and female

Butterfly — some have one female wing and one male wing

Kangaroo — males show affection toward other males

Goat — most males have close connections with other males, many do not become parents; a high percentage have a body that is both male and female

Deer — some have a body that is both male and female; both males and some females have horns, both lose them for part of the year; those with half and half coloring are both male and female

and more! this is just a small sampling of nature's immense diversity!

Mushrooms have thousands of different body types beyond male and female

Snails have a body that is both male and female and can switch back and forth

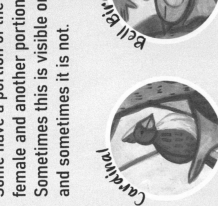

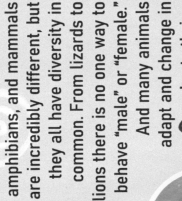
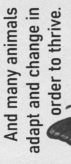

©2023 Maya Gonzalez | *The Gender and Infinity Book for Kids* | WWW.GENDERWHEEL.COM

Finding your way

STEP 1 LEARN about the patterns of abundant body, gender, and relationship diversity across all realms of nature.

LEARN ABOUT PLANTS

In nature there are lots of different kinds of bodies

LEARN ABOUT AQUATIC LIFE

In nature there are lots of different ways to reproduce

LEARN ABOUT BIRDS

In nature there are lots of different ways to feel and behave

LEARN ABOUT AMPHIBIANS REPTILES + MAMMALS

Diversity keeps nature Strong

LEARN ABOUT PEOPLE

STEP 2 SEE how the two boxes have been overlaid onto everything, erasing nature's patterns of diversity and impacting our ability to fully understand the world and ourselves.

©2023 Maya Gonzalez | *The Gender and Infinity Book for Kids* | WWW.GENDERWHEEL.COM

STEP 3 EXPAND out of the boxes in how you think and talk and return to nature's infinite circles and cycles of diversity.

BEING your truest, most unique self is important because you are a part of the great flow of never ending diversity in the world.

Back to Nature

...AND TO BEING YOUR FULLEST SELF!

Everyone everywhere, inside and outside, is a part of infinity...Going.

Gender Wheel®

The Gender and Infinity Book for Kids is based on the Gender Wheel.

The Gender Wheel is an educational tool that centers nature and helps us understand body, gender, and relationship diversity.

Through its design and motion the Gender Wheel provides a way for us to make sense out of big concepts like infinite diversity and nature's constant flow, as well as our unique place in all of it.

The Gender Wheel consists of 4 concentric circles around a center star.

Each circle is a continuum and holds infinite possibilities. Each circle also rotates creating infinite interactive possibilities between the circles.

Shown here is a very simple representation of the Wheel. You can see it in detail and learn more at:

WWW.GENDERWHEEL.COM/ABOUT

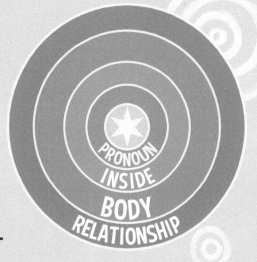

PRONOUN
INSIDE
BODY
RELATIONSHIP

©2023 Maya Gonzalez | *The Gender and Infinity Book for Kids* | WWW.GENDERWHEEL.COM

When you were born you became a part of all this.

How do we be our truest self in the midst of THE BOXES?

#1 NATURE-BASED

We use the reality of nature to know that body, gender, and relationship diversity are normal, necessary, and valuable to the whole.

The path on the previous page shows us the way. It is the same path we see weave through the book. The process is rooted in the main principles of the Gender Wheel which in turn rise from seeing nature's timeless patterns.

#2 DECOLONIZED

We stay aware of the presence and pressure to conform to two boxes and how they've been overlaid onto nature, erasing and limiting its diversity.

Being & Belonging

By continuously cycling through the 3 step process, we can be aware of the boxes' impact while strengthening our sense of belonging, our necessity, and the value of our truest self as well as everyone else's.

Gender Wheel Process & Principles

#3 HOLISTIC

We shift how we think and talk to consistently include nature's vast body, gender, and relationship diversity.

Back to Nature
Note to Adults

Did you notice the one word in the title that is never mentioned in the story? Gender. While we are addressing gender, we're doing it outside of how we tend to think and talk about gender. We are diving below human definitions and identities to a deeper understanding of what bodies and gender mean within the context of all of nature.

Familiar terms like female and male are used in the back to talk about the physicality of bodies in nature. Similarly, the familiar terms, girl and boy boxes, are used to talk about what has been overlaid onto bodies. We don't want to identify kids by their assigned boxes, but we do want to be able to acknowledge their bodies in order to see their authentic selves beyond assigned boxes.

As all realms of nature confirm, there are infinite ways to feel inside infinite bodies, but it will take time to move away from the boxes. By bringing familiar words with us on the path, we can create bridges into new ways of thinking and eventually new language while breaking free from gender assignments.

They want to know because THE BOX isn't just about the body a person is born with.

It is also about how that body is expected to look, act and feel inside, even how that person is treated.

The point is to help kids see both the inside and outside self within the reality of nature's infinite diversity. This highlights the value of letting the authentic self BE, while lessening the pressure to conform to the boxes. This frees nature's infinity.

The art of the story provides an immediate nonverbal connection, while the information in the back is there to expand the understanding of the animals and the kids on the next read and the next. Repetition helps deepen the story and unwind the impact of the boxes.

The Gender Wheel is based on nature's timeless patterns with multiple healing modalities embedded in the approach. Because we have all been affected by gender oppression, it calls in generational healing. It will take time, but nature is there to hold us and show us the path through.

©2023 Maya Gonzalez | *The Gender and Infinity Book for Kids* | WWW.GENDERWHEEL.COM

Quick Tips

NATURE-BASED

1 DIG DEEPER The research is piling up and it turns out nature's secret power is diversity. And it's not just people. It's all living beings. Plants, fish, birds, animals. Everything, including you, is a part of the timeless patterns of nature's body, gender, and relationship diversity. But it can be hard to find. Many institutions, programs, zoos and more don't update their information to include this kind of diversity. We know it exists. If you don't see it, investigate! We can educate ourselves and our kids.

DECOLONIZED

2 UNEARTH UNIQUENESS All kids (and adults) experience pressure to conform to the boxes. This contributes to stress, bullying, behavior problems, depression, learning issues and more. If we want to see the world and ourselves as we really are, we need to see infinity in our uniqueness. We do this by removing our own assumptions and expectations about who we think people can be based on the boxes. This helps transform the constant pressure to conform in the world around us. We want everybody to be free to be exactly who they are, just like in nature.

HOLISTIC

3 PLANT SEEDS To make lasting change we need new ways to think and talk about bodies and gender that include everyone all of the time. Fortunately when we center nature's infinite body and gender diversity, we start to move away from limited binary thinking toward a more holistic path. This is strengthened by learning more about nature's circles, cycles, and continuums like those of the Gender Wheel. We complete the circle when we engage gender-inclusive language.

Find additional resources that support these quick tips on our website:
WWW.GENDERWHEEL.COM/INFINITY-TIPS

More Gender Wheel books!

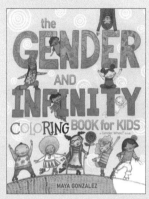

The Gender and Infinity COLORING Book for Kids

They She He Me: Free to Be!

They, She, He easy as ABC

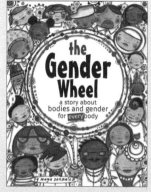

The Gender Wheel: a story about bodies and gender for every body

Educational Tools

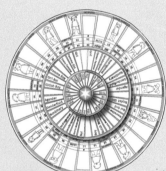

Playing with Pronouns Educational Card Deck, Make the Gender Wheel Project, Lesson Plans, Coloring Pages and more! Get to know the kids from this book and their whole community of friends across all of our books and materials!

Learn More

Facilitated Workshops & Professional Development Trainings EXPLORE a nature-based, decolonized, and holistic perspective of gender. LEARN practical skills to interrupt systemic gender oppression, build greater personal resilience, and create healing genderFULL environments.

WWW.GENDERWHEEL.COM

Maya Gonzalez is an award-winning children's book artist, author, educator, and publisher who has always been inspired by the healing power of nature! Maya has created more than thirty kids books with many more on the way. Maya lives with their family in the wild, wild woods of San Francisco by the blue, blue sea full of whales. www.mayagonzalez.com

Deepest love and respect for Matthew and the wisdom and presence he brings to our life and our work together. I literally couldn't/wouldn't without you. And BIG LOVE FOREVER for Sky and Zai
—M.G.

Text & Illustrations Copyright © 2023 by Maya Gonzalez

Published by Gender Wheel, an imprint of Reflection Press,
San Francisco, CA since 2009
The *Gender Wheel*® was created by Maya Gonzalez
and is a registered trademark of Reflection Press

All rights reserved. No part of this book may be reproduced or transmitted in any form or by any means, electronic, mechanical, photocopying, recording, or otherwise, without prior written permission of the publisher.

ISBN 978-1-945289-22-4 (hardcover)
ISBN 978-1-945289-23-1 (paperback)
ISBN 978-1-945289-27-9 (coloring book)
Library of Congress Control Number: 2023946765
Consultation, Book Design & Production by Matthew S.G.

Summary: Not your average book about gender! A kid's guide to BEING your fullest self using the stunning and infinite reflection of nature to burst OUT of the boxes that limit ALL of us.

The Gender Wheel® books rise from the Gender Wheel®Approach, a nature-based, decolonized, and holistic approach to gender. Inclusive perspectives and practices at every level of the approach support a strong sense of self, while creating systemic change in the world at large.

Reflection Press is a POC queer and trans owned independent publisher of radical and revolutionary children's books and works that expand cultural and spiritual awareness. Rooted in holistic, nature-based, and anti-oppression frameworks, our materials support a strong sense of individuality along with a community model of real inclusion. Visit us at **www.reflectionpress.com** and **www.genderwheel.com**

For permissions, bulk orders, or if you receive defective or misprinted books, please contact us at info@reflectionpress.com

Printed in the USA
CPSIA information can be obtained
at www.ICGtesting.com
LVHW060954161123
R17968700002B/R179687PG763432LVX00001B/1